The Two of Them Are Pretty Much Like This
2
story and art by
Takashi Ikeda
D1178500

Contents

Chapter 25

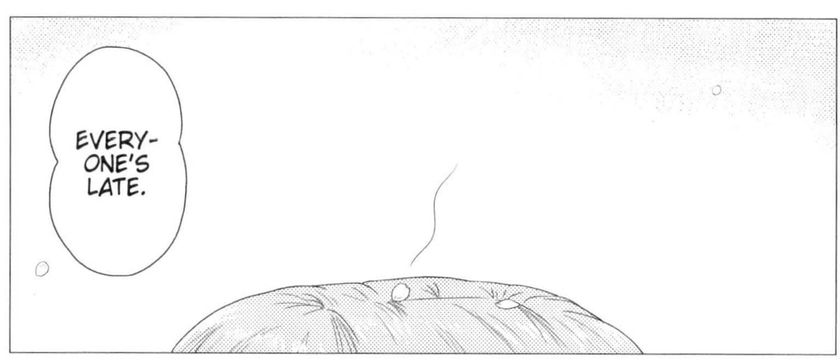

THE PETALS ARE FALLING.

HAVE I GOT STATIC CLING OR SOME-THING?
MAYBE YOU'VE GOT A LITTLE CHERRY BLOSSOM FAIRY?

ME AGAIN?

COME ON, SAKUMA.
SERIOUSLY?
HOW CAN YOU SAY THAT SO NONCHA-LANTLY?
HA HA HA!
IT'S MY JOB.
GOTTA BE ABLE TO SAY CHEESY LINES SHAMELESSLY.

EVERY-ONE'S SO LATE.
YEAH, SERI-OUSLY.

I SHOULD HAVE BROUGHT ANOTHER BOOK.

AHA!
I DIDN'T NOTICE THE PETALS BECAUSE I COULDN'T SEE THE TOP OF YOUR HAT!
ズバーーン
BAAAM

ざっ
SWIP

WHAT?
I'M STAND-ING GUARD!
I DON'T WANT PETALS TO FALL ON YOU.

OKAY?
PROTECT ME FROM THE PETALS, THEN.
JUST LEAVE IT TO ME!

SHE ENDED UP BE-COMING A SHIELD.
EVERYONE SURE IS TAKING THEIR TIME.
DID WE GO TO THE WRONG SPOT?
NO, THAT CAN'T BE IT ...

OH?
Chapter 26

SAKUMA, YOU USED TO...
HAVE PIERCED EARS, RIGHT?
YEAH.

BUT THE HOLES CLOSED UP...
BECAUSE I WAS TOO LAZY TO PUT ON EARRINGS.
HUH... SO, THE HOLES DO CLOSE UP.

WHAT? YOU WANT TO GET YOUR EARS PIERCED?
NAH. I DON'T LIKE PAIN, SO I'LL PASS.
BRUSH BRUSH BRUSH

AH!
YOU'RE THINKING THAT I'M BEING A BABY, AREN'T YOU?!
IT'S JUST MY PERSONAL PHILOSOPHY! YOU KNOW, IT'S, *UH*...WHAT WAS IT AGAIN? THAT QUOTE ABOUT NOT HARMING YOUR INTERNAL ORGANS OR WHATEVER.
FILIAL PIETY BEGINS WITH NOT HARMING THE BODY OUR PARENTS GAVE US?
YEAH THAT!
HMM...

カチャ
KA-CHAK
PEEL

バヂッ
KA-THUNK
ビクウッ
TWITCH

ぐっ…
GRIP
CLENCH
ぐぐぐ…

SST
ぴゅっ
WHOOSH

KA-
THUNK
PEEK

SST
ぴゅっ
WHOOSH

WANNA GIVE IT A TRY?

ひくっ
TWITCH

SHE'S THAT SCARED, HUH?
ぴゅっ
WHOOSH
TREMBLE TREMBLE

BE GENTLE WITH ME... OKAY?
HERE I GO! READY?
BREATHE IN, AND THEN BREATHE OUT.
THERE!
THAT'S WHAT I'LL SAY WHEN I DO IT.
COME ON! DON'T SCARE ME LIKE THAT!
KA-THUNK
EEP!

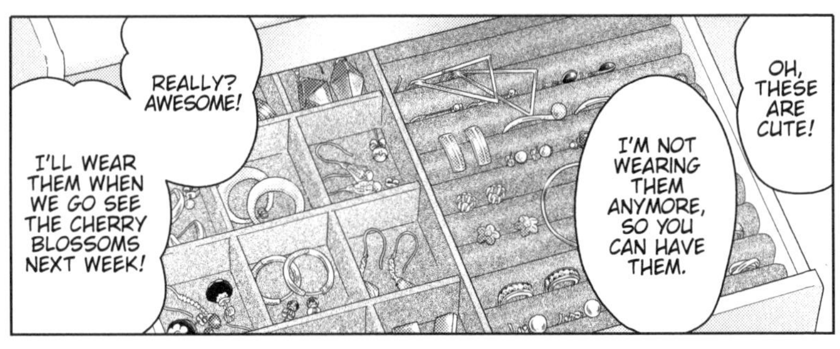

SO WE BOTH HAVE MATCHING EARRINGS.

Chapter 27

OH!

THEY'RE HERE!

IT GOT SO CROWD-ED.
WHO SAID THAT THIS WAS A NICE "SECRET" SPOT?
THEY PROBABLY ALL THOUGHT IT WAS A NICE SECRET SPOT.
WHAT? THIS GIRL IS MIHO-CHAN?!
WELL, IT HAPPENS.
UH, ANYWAY ...
LET'S MAKE A TOAST TO WAKO-CHAN PASSING THE AUDITION!
WAIT...
CHEERS!
THIS IS WEIRD...
DIDN'T WE DO THIS THE OTHER DAY?

VSSSH
VSSSH

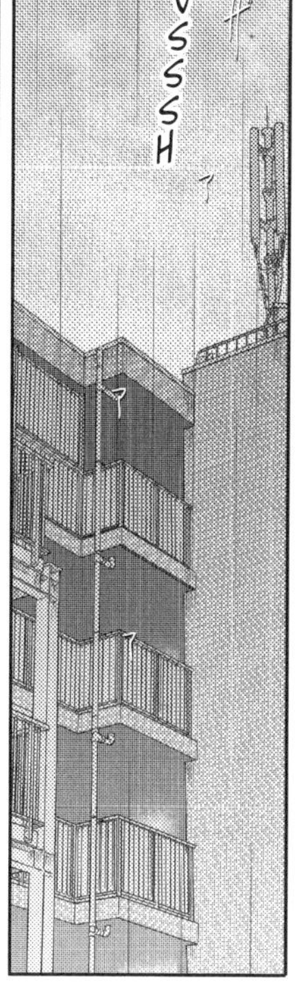
VSSSH

VSSSH

IT'S POUR-ING.
カララ…
RATTLE

IT'S FINE. THERE'S ALWAYS NEXT YEAR.

Chapter 28

HMM

ARGH

YOU'RE STILL HERE?
WON'T YOU BE IN TROUBLE IF YOU'RE LATE FOR YOUR FIRST INTERVIEW?
I-I DON'T LOOK WEIRD, DO I?!
DO I LOOK GOOD WITH THESE EARRINGS?!

YEAH. YOU LOOK SUPER DUPER CUTE.
OK OK!
OH, COME ON! THAT'S NOT HELPFUL AT ALL!

I'M GOING!
SEEE YA!
DAMMIT!
THAT SURE...
TAKES ME BACK.
WHEN I FIRST WORE EARRINGS...
バタン!
THUD
FWSH
WHAT WAS IT LIKE AGAIN?
WAIT...
WHEN DID I EVEN GET MY EARS PIERCED IN THE FIRST PLACE?
HUH...

Mary Pompon
¥4,000
Mary Pompon
¥5,500

SWIP SWIP
ちょい ちょい
HMM ...
SIIIP

I GUESS IT'D BE BETTER ...
TO GO TO THE STORE WITH HER IN PERSON...
OH, BUT SHE MIGHT BE HAPPY TO GET A PRESENT.
CHOCO PIE

MUNCH

CLACK
THERE!
ORDER PLACED!

HA HA HA!
IT WON'T HURT TO BUY A BUNCH OF THEM.
RIIING
ピロロロロロッ

HELLO? OH, HI!
HUH? AH, YES! YES!
EVERYTHING'S GOING GREAT! YES! YES! OH YEAH! *HA HA HA HA HA...*

はあーっ
HAAAAH...
GLOOM

OKAY, WE'LL TAKE A GROUP PHOTO TO WRAP THIS UP.
EVERYONE, PLEASE GET READY!
OKAY!

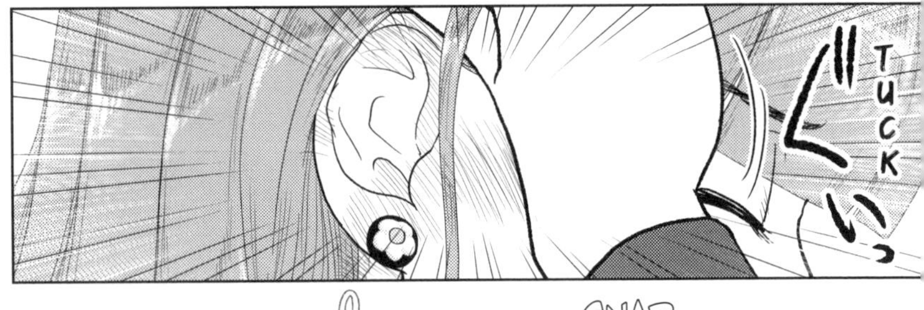
TUCK

SNAP

SAKUMA'S JOURNEY

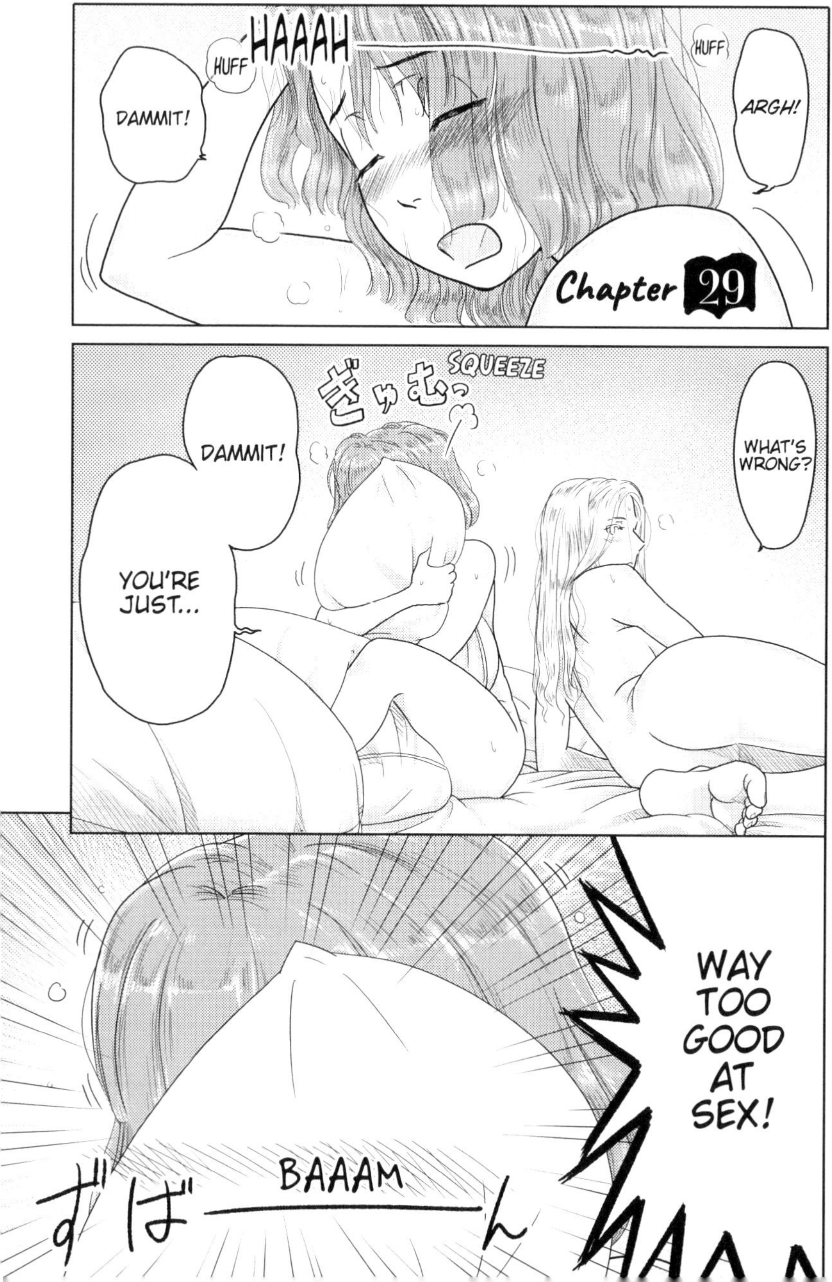

Chapter 29

WHAT'S WRONG?
ぎゅむっ
SQUEEZE
DAMMIT!
YOU'RE JUST...

WAY TOO GOOD AT SEX!
ずば――ん
BAAAM

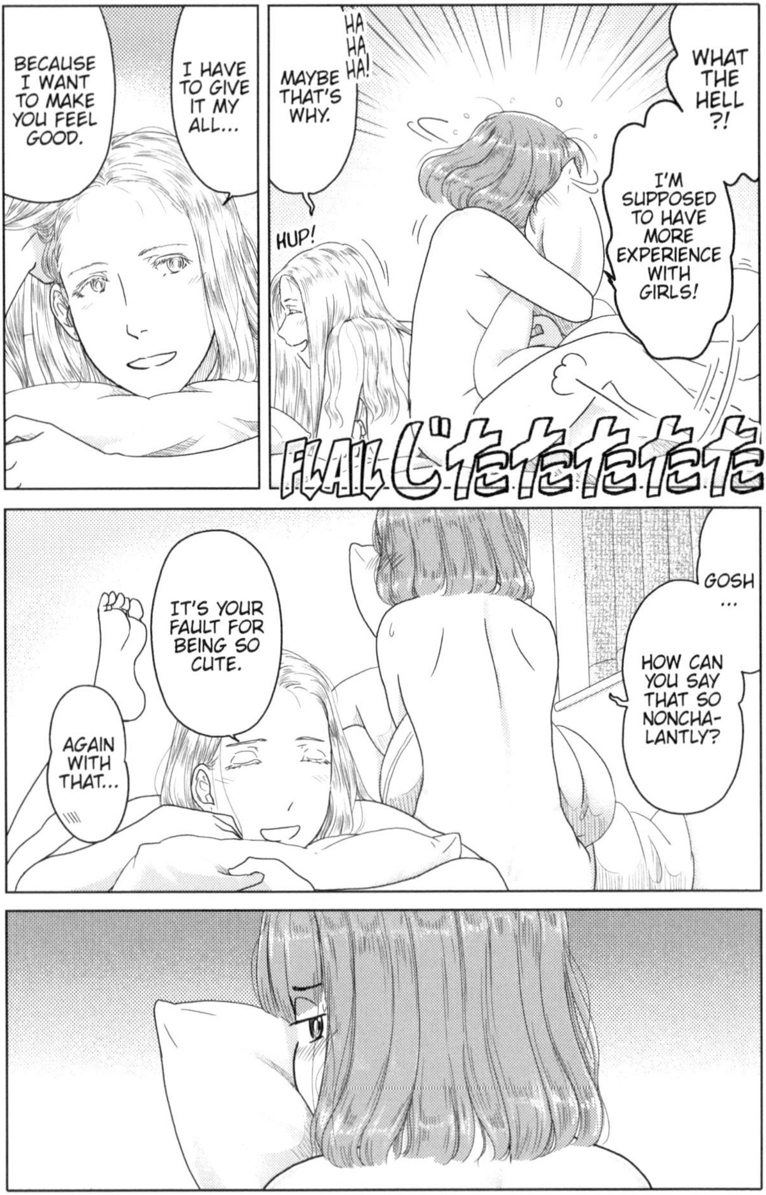

WHAT THE HELL?!

I'M SUPPOSED TO HAVE MORE EXPERIENCE WITH GIRLS!

HA HA HA!

MAYBE THAT'S WHY.

HUP!

FLAIL じたたたたた

I HAVE TO GIVE IT MY ALL...

BECAUSE I WANT TO MAKE YOU FEEL GOOD.

GOSH...

HOW CAN YOU SAY THAT SO NONCHA-LANTLY?

IT'S YOUR FAULT FOR BEING SO CUTE.

AGAIN WITH THAT...

YOU WERE ...
VERY CUTE WHEN YOU CAME, TOO.

MUTTER MUTTER
HMM?
WHAT IS IT?
MUMBLE ぶつ
MUMBLE ぶつ

PUFF

PFFT...
HEH HEH...

HEY!
I'M BEING SERI-OUS!
SORRY.
IT'S JUST THAT ...

GRRR

YOU REALLY MEAN IT?

YEAH!
がば
FWAP
I'M A CUTE GIRL?
YUP! YOU TOTALLY ARE!

YOU'RE VERY CUTE, SAKUMA.
I LOVE YOU.

どさっ…
THUMP
HEH HEH...

EEEEEK!

OH DEAR! UMM...
EXCUSE ME, UH...PERSON WHO LIVES IN APARTMENT 309!
Chapter 30

カララ… RATTLE
MEW!
MEW!

MEEEW!

I'LL COME DOWN THERE TO GET MY CAT RIGHT NOW!
MEW!
MEW!
IT'LL RUN AWAY IF YOU DO ANYTHING, SO JUST LEAVE IT BE!
I'M SO, SO SORRY ABOUT THIS!
IT WON'T TAKE LONG!
SORRY IT'S A BIT MESSY IN HERE ...
COME ON IN.
NO, IT'S OKAY!
THANKS FOR LETTING ME IN!
SST
HUH?
IT WAS ON THE FUTON A MOMENT AGO...
WHAT ?!

KINAKO-CHAN!
RATTLE
DASH
AH!
HEY!
KINAKO-CHAN, STOP!
QUICK! CLOSE ALL THE WINDOWS!
KINAKO-CHAN, THIS ISN'T OUR APARTMENT!
COME ON, GET BACK HERE!
UH...
UM...
WON'T YOU SCARE IT IF YOU KEEP YELLING?
OH!
YOU'RE RIGHT!
SNEAK
SNEAK

I CAN REACH IT WITHOUT A CHAIR …

CLATTER

OH, MOVE A BIT CLOSER TO THE MIDDLE. IT'S NOT SAFE…

NO, PLEASE, DON'T TROUBLE YOURSELF!

COME ON, KINAKO-CHAN! IT'S OKAY! DON'T BE SCARED…

HISS…

OW!
EEP!
CLATTER
THUMP
OUCH...
ARE YOU OKAY?
WAAAAH!

S...
S-S-S-S-SORRY ABOUT THAT!
I'LL BE SURE TO PAY YOU FOR THE DAMAGED FUTON!
どばぁん
BWAM
っぴゅ
WHOOSH
FWOP
ひょこっ
MEW!
HUH?
SHE SOMEHOW MANAGED TO CATCH THE CAT LATER.

Chapter 31

AS AN APOLOGY FOR THE COMMOTION THE OTHER DAY...

SHE INVITED SAKUMA AND WANKO OVER FOR TEA.

DO YOU LIKE TO WATCH MOVIES?

KINAKO IS TOO SHY TO COME OUT.

IN MODERATION, YEAH.

WOW, A PROJECTOR!

I HOPE YOU GET TO WRITE FOR A MOVIE ONE DAY, SAKUMA!

YOU'RE IN THAT BUSINESS?

WHOA!

TMP TMP TMP TMP TMP
TMP TMP TMP TMP TMP

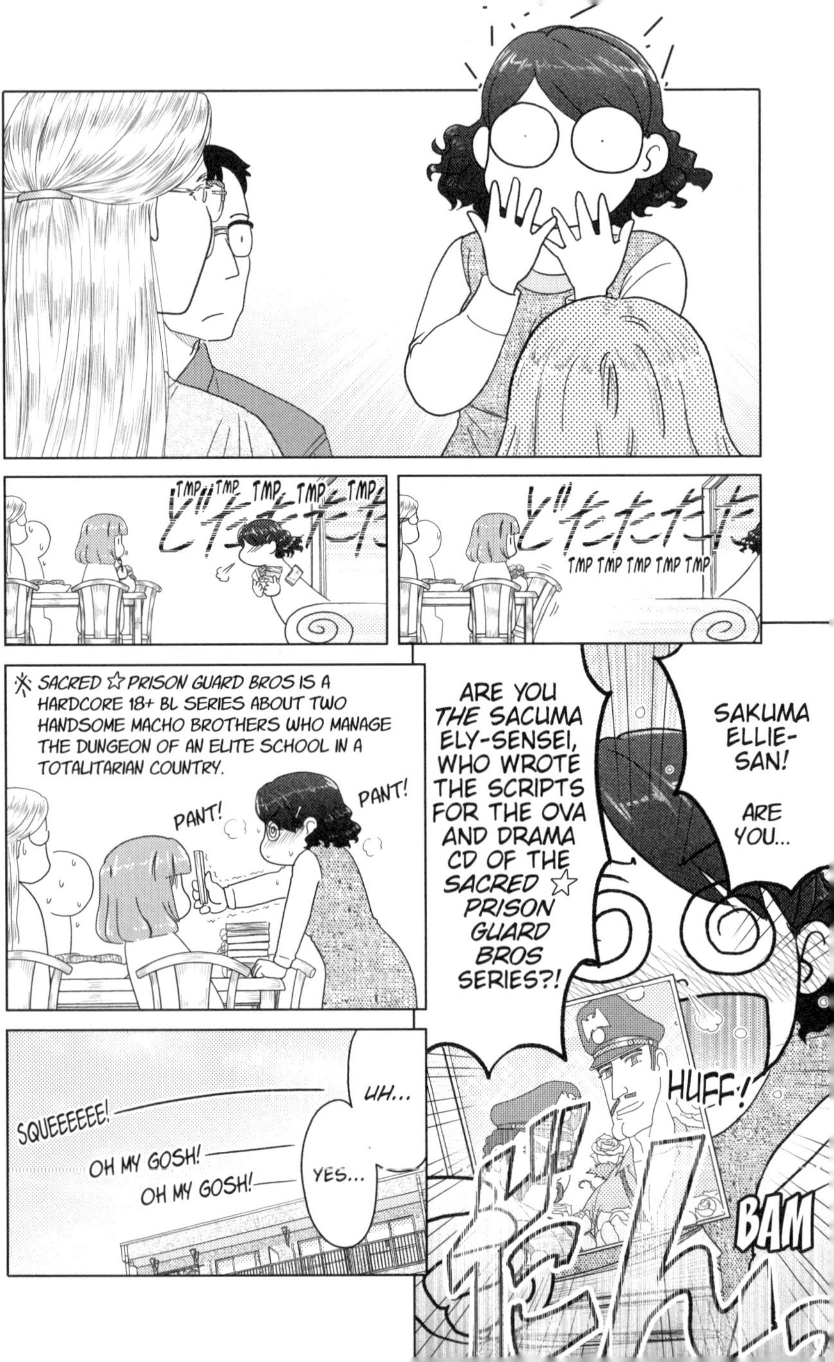

SAKUMA ELLIE-SAN!

ARE YOU...
ARE YOU *THE* SACUMA ELY-SENSEI, WHO WROTE THE SCRIPTS FOR THE OVA AND DRAMA CD OF THE *SACRED ☆ PRISON GUARD BROS* SERIES?!
HUFF!
BAM

※ *SACRED ☆ PRISON GUARD BROS* IS A HARDCORE 18+ BL SERIES ABOUT TWO HANDSOME MACHO BROTHERS WHO MANAGE THE DUNGEON OF AN ELITE SCHOOL IN A TOTALITARIAN COUNTRY.
PANT!
PANT!

UH...
YES...
SQUEEEEEE!
OH MY GOSH!
OH MY GOSH!

SO, YOU LIKE BL?
HUH?
THIS CAKE IS SO GOOD!
OH, YES! ESPECIALLY THIS SERIES!
GIVING HER AN AUTO-GRAPH.
THANK YOU!
I HAVE ALL THE MERCH AND WENT TO ALL THE EVENTS!
MUST'VE BEEN HARD TO GO TO THEM ALL, SINCE SOME WERE OUT IN THE COUNTRY.
I JUST LOVE IT THAT MUCH!
HERE YOU GO.
WOOOW!
OH!
D-DO YOU WANT TO TAKE A LOOK AT MY COLLECTION ?!
UH...
SURE, I GUESS.
FWIP
HUFF!
I-I'LL TAKE YOU TO MY BEDROOM!

THIS IS YOUR BED-ROOM?
WOW!
IS YOUR HUSBAND OKAY WITH THIS?
YUP! HE'S TOTALLY COOL WITH IT!
THIS POSTER WAS WITHDRAWN AFTER THREE DAYS.
YOU EVEN HAVE THE PROMO-TIONAL ITEMS FOR THE GAME.
AMAZING.
YOU CAN GET THEM FROM ONLINE AUCTIONS NOWA-DAYS!
OH, A KAN DOLL.
ARE THOSE TWO THE SAME?
OH, THIS ONE HAS CHEST HAIR.

BY THE WAY...
CAN YOU KEEP SACUMA ELY'S ADDRESS A SECRET?
HUH?
OH, OF COURSE! I WON'T TELL A SOUL!
CAW
CAW
THANK YOU FOR THE WONDERFUL TEA.
COME AGAIN ANY TIME.
SENSEI!
PLEASE TAKE THIS! IT WAS SENT FROM MY HOMETOWN!
UH, WE'RE NEIGHBORS, SO CAN YOU NOT CALL ME SENSEI?
IT JUST FEELS WEIRD.
HUH?
OH, OKAY! SORRY ABOUT THAT!
I'LL KEEP AN EYE OUT FOR THE NEW INSTALLMENT OF THE *SACRED ☆ PRISON GUARD BROS* SERIES!
IT'S NOT UP TO ME...
I'LL BE SURE TO CHECK OUT YOUR OTHER WORKS, TOO, SENSEI!
WAIT, NOT SENSEI!
CALM DOWN, MADOKA-SAN.
TMP
TMP

I'LL CARRY IT FOR YOU.

Chapter 32

GOOD MORNING!

HELLO! NICE WEATHER, HUH?

ARE YOU GOING ON AN OUTING? TAKE CARE!

I'M GLAD YOU HAVE A NICE NEIGHBOR.
AND NOT SOME DANGEROUS FANGIRL.
SHE'S KINDA SCARY, THOUGH.
YEAH, BUT...

DOESN'T HER HUSBAND LOOK KIND OF TIRED?
GOOD MORNING.
OH, HELLO.
YOU'RE ON YOUR OWN TODAY?
YEAH. I'VE GOT SOME WORK TO DO.
SO, YOU DON'T JUST WRITE SCRIPTS AT HOME, HUH?
AN INBOUND TRAIN WILL ARRIVE SOON.
I DO HAVE TO GET OUT OF MY APARTMENT A LOT, FOR MEETINGS AND RECORDING SESSIONS AND WHATNOT.
FOR YOUR SAFETY, PLEASE STAY BEHIND THE WHITE LINE.
I'M JUST A CONTRACTOR ON PROJECTS, SO BEING CALLED SENSEI DOESN'T FEEL RIGHT.
HA HA HA.

SIGH...

HAS MADO-KA-SAN...
BEEN CAUSING TROUBLE FOR YOU BECAUSE OF ME?

NO.
NOT AT ALL.

LET'S JUST SAY SHE HAS MORE THINGS TO FANGIRL OVER NOW.
EVERY DAY HAS BECOME MORE FUN FOR HER, SO AS HER HUSBAND, THAT MAKES ME HAPPY TOO.

YOU TWO SURE ARE CLOSE.
OH, NO.
WE'RE NOT AS CLOSE AS YOU AND YOUR GIRLFRIEND ARE.

DIIING DIIING
AN INBOUND TRAIN IS ARRIVING.
PLEASE STAY BEHIND THE WHITE LINE.
OKAY, THE TRAIN'S COMING.

FWOOOOO
HOOONK

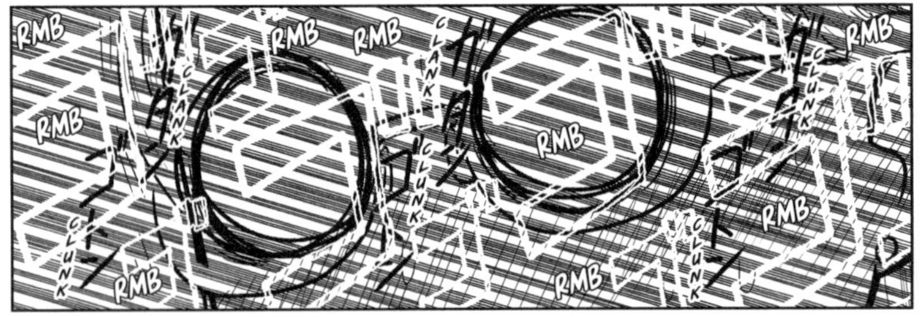
RMB
CLANK
CLUNK
CLUNK

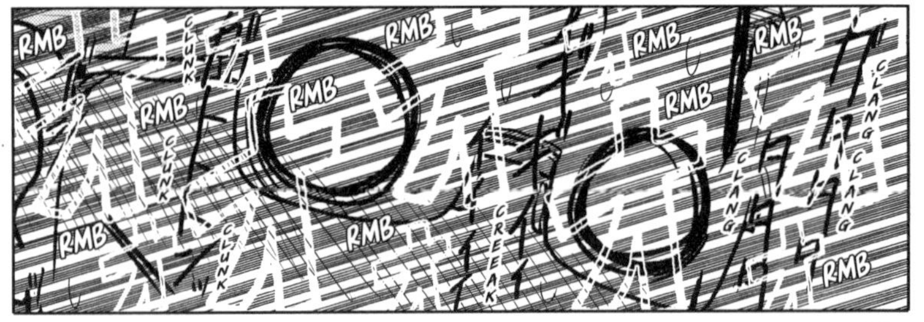
RMB
CLUNK
CLANG
CREEAK

WE'LL TRY TO...
KEEP OUR VOICES DOWN.
PLATFORM B. PLATFORM B.
DIIING
MADOKA-SAN...
DOES SEEM TO LOVE IT, THOUGH.
SHE THINKS OF IT AS A REWARD...
OH!
WELCOME HOME, SAKUMA!
LOOK AT THIS FUTON!
IT'S THE REPLACEMENT FOR THE ONE THE CAT DAMAGED!
PAT PAT
SHE COULD'VE JUST GOTTEN US A NEW COVER.
MAN, IT SURE IS NICE TO HAVE FANS. ♫
I CAN UNPACK IT NOW, RIGHT? OKAY, LET'S DO THIS! ♪
RIP RIP

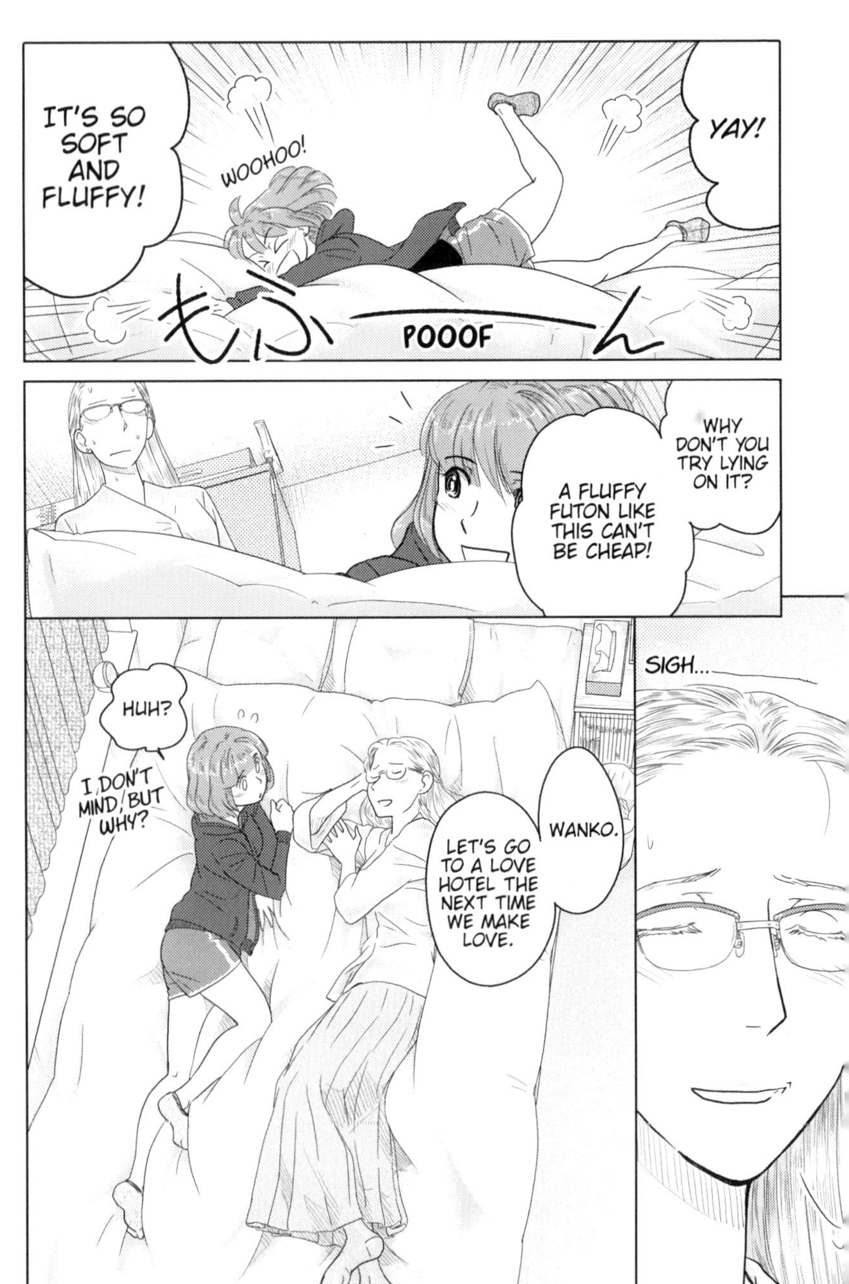
YAY!
WOOHOO!
IT'S SO SOFT AND FLUFFY!
もふーーん
POOOF
WHY DON'T YOU TRY LYING ON IT?
A FLUFFY FUTON LIKE THIS CAN'T BE CHEAP!
SIGH...
WANKO.
LET'S GO TO A LOVE HOTEL THE NEXT TIME WE MAKE LOVE.
HUH?
I DON'T MIND, BUT WHY?

Chapter 33

GOOD MORNING. I'M NEMORI KYOKO, THE VOICE ACTRESS OF RYUDOU AKANE.
I'LL DO ALL I CAN TO SUPPORT MY SISTERS AS THE ELDEST SISTER.
I'M OU MIREI FROM OFFICE 90. I'LL BE VOICING RYUDOU SUBA-RU.
I'LL DO MY BEST TO VOICE HER FOR ALL THIRTEEN EPI-SODES.
I'M INUZUKA WAKO FROM AOTA ENTER-PRISE!
I'LL BE VOICING RYUDOU SUBARU! I MEAN MIDORI!
I'M STILL A ROOKIE, SO I HOPE I CAN LEARN FROM ALL OF JYUU!
FWIP
SHE TRIPPED OVER HER WORDS.
SHE'S SO INNOCENT.

*A pun on Mirei's surname, meaning 'puppy.'

AL☆PACA
WOW!
AN ALPACA, HUH?
HEY!
WANKO-CHAN! HOW AM I SUPPOSED TO REACT TO THAT?
DROOP

A-ALPACAS ARE PRETTY COOL!
THEY'RE FLUFFY, AND ALSO SNAZZY!
ARE YOU SERIOUS?
I'VE NEVER HEARD ANYONE SAY ALPACAS ARE COOL BEFORE.

I'M SO, SOOO...

SORRY!

NIGHT HAD FALLEN.

WELL, THIS IS THE FIRST TIME YOU HAVE A MAIN ROLE, WAKO-CHAN.

TODAY IS JUST A MINI-DRAMA FOR AN EVENT, NOT THE ACTUAL SHOW.

YEAH. WE WERE ALL READY FOR A STORM OF RETAKES.

AL-PACAS...
THAT'S WHAT YOU'RE SORRY ABOUT?!
FWISH

I'LL COME UP WITH A MORE FITTING ANIMAL FOR YOU BY NEXT WEEK!
FWIP
んぱっ
THERE'S NO NEED.
JUST GIVE IT A REST ALREADY.

KYOKO JUST WANTED THE TWO OF YOU TO GET ALONG. RIGHT?
YEAH. I WAS BEING CONSIDER-ATE IN MY OWN WAY.
I'M (VOICING) THE BIG SISTER, AFTER ALL.

ACTU-ALLY...

LOOM

すいっ

!

Chapter 34

COUGH COUGH COUGH
COUGH COUGH

WHAT THE HELL?!

YOU SEE...

BLAH BLAH

YADDA YADDA

I SHOULDN'T HAVE ASKED...

DIIING

J-J...
JUST GOOGLE IT!
YOU HAVE A SMARTPHONE, DON'T YOU?
SMARTPHONES ARE HANDY THAT WAY!
OH, RIGHT.

Google
Love hotels for girls

OH, THEY DO ALLOW GIRLS TO GO TOGETHER ...
BUT IT'S MAINLY FOR GIRLS-ONLY PARTIES.

HMM. NOW'S AN IMPORTANT TIME FOR HER CAREER. IT MIGHT CAUSE A SCANDAL.

WELL, I'M GLAD IT'S...
GOING SO WELL FOR YOU TWO.

GOSH, THIS IS EMBAR-RASSING.
SO UNBECOMING FOR SOME-ONE MY AGE.
WANKO-CHAN SURE IS AMAZING, THOUGH.

SHE MANAGED TO MAKE A STRAIGHT GIRL LIKE YOU FALL MADLY IN LOVE WITH HER.
NO, STOP IT! DON'T SAY THAT!
YOU'RE GOING TO CRY ABOUT IT LATER! DON'T SAY IT!
THORN
YOU HAVE TO WONDER HOW MANY WOMEN SHE'S BEEN WITH.
AH, SHE SAID IT.
WHATEVER. I DON'T CARE ANYMORE.

HUH?
YOU DON'T CARE ABOUT HER PAST GIRLFRIENDS? OR WHO WAS HER FIRST?
DOES IT NOT BOTHER YOU?
NOPE. NOT AT ALL.
MUNCH MUNCH

THE FUTURE IS ALL THAT MATTERS FOR BOTH OF US.

CRACK

JEEZ, COULD YOU BE ANY MORE LOVEY-DOVEY?

HA HA HA! WAS THAT TOO CHEESY?

BUT YOU KNOW, THIS IS BASICALLY AN OCCUPATIONAL DISEASE FOR US.

IT'S LIKE A CONTEST WHERE WE SAY CHEESY LINES WHILE TRYING TO KEEP A STRAIGHT FACE!

MAYBE I SHOULD JUST GO HOME...

WANKO ALSO...

BLUSHES WHEN SHE HEARS MY CHEESY LINES, AND IT'S JUST SO CUTE.

SO, IT'S PRETTY MUCH A HABIT FOR ME NOW.

OH, WHAT AM I TO DO?

CRACK

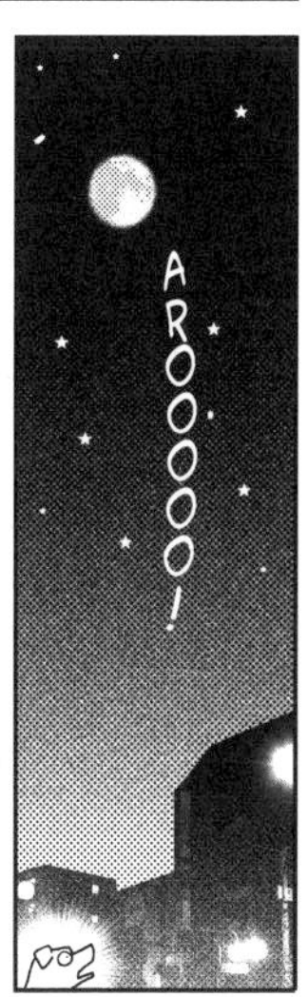

笑う
アイツの
かわいさと
きたらァーー
SHE'S JUST SO DAMN CUTE...
WHEN SHE SMILES!
O...
OKAY?
ジジ…
ZREE ZREE

SUZUKAKE MIHO (23) WORKS FOR AOTA ENTERPRISE.

SHE BECAME A TRAINEE AROUND THE SAME TIME AS WANKO, BUT HAD A BIT MORE WORK.

Chapter 35

FLICK

SSSHH
WHIIIR
SPLISH
SPLISH

DIIING

SLURP
VIDEO FOR REHEARSAL.

BRRRRR
BRRRRRR
BRRRRRR
Mom

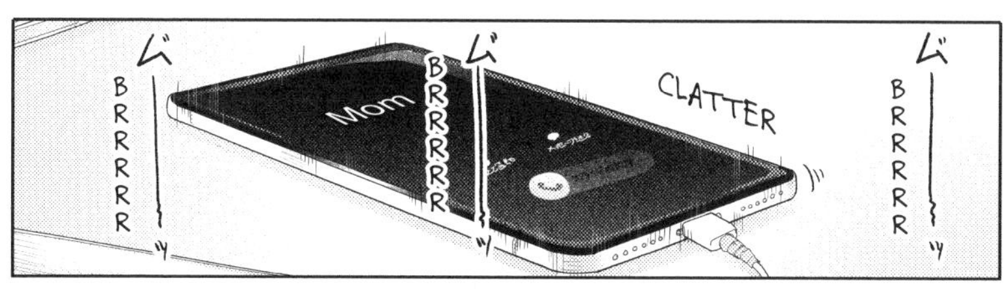
BRRRRR
Mom
BRRRRR
CLATTER
BRRRRR

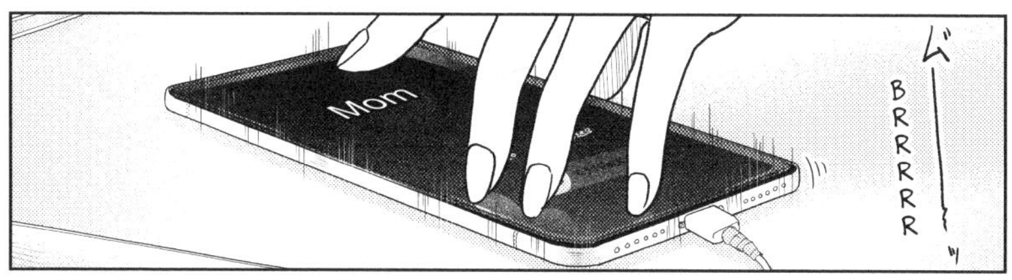
Mom
BRRRRR

HELLO.
NO, I'M EATING DINNER RIGHT NOW.

NO, I WAS AT MY PART-TIME JOB.
TAP
TAP
AT THE CONVE-NIENCE STORE, YEAH.

UH, YEAH.
NAH, I DUNNO 'BOUT THAT.

NO, THE VOICE ACTING THING.
I'VE BEEN GOING TO AUDITIONS AND ALL.
I'VE BEEN GETTING DECENT WORK, TOO.
VIDEO GAMES AND WHATNOT. I DID A DRAMA CD RECENTLY, TOO.
IT'S FOR COMPANIES. YOU CAN LISTEN TO IT ONLINE. I TEXTED YOU 'BOUT IT.
SHAKE ゆっさ
SHAKE ゆっさ
SHAKE ゆっさ

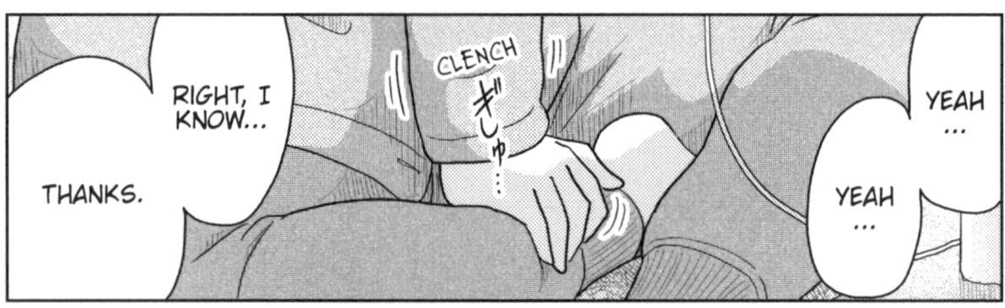

WHEW...

HUFF!
HUFF!

CHEEP CHEEP CHEEP

SHE SELLS SEA-SHELLS BY THE SEA SHORE...
SHE SELLS SEA-SHELLS BY THE SEA SHORE...
SHE'S WORKING HARD TODAY, TOO.

OH.
IT'S THAT DRAMA CD I DID.

WHIIIR
I WONDER IF IT'LL GET AN ANIME.
IT DOES SEEM TO BE A HIT, SO MAYBE?
CLUNK
CLUNK
CLUNK
CLUNK

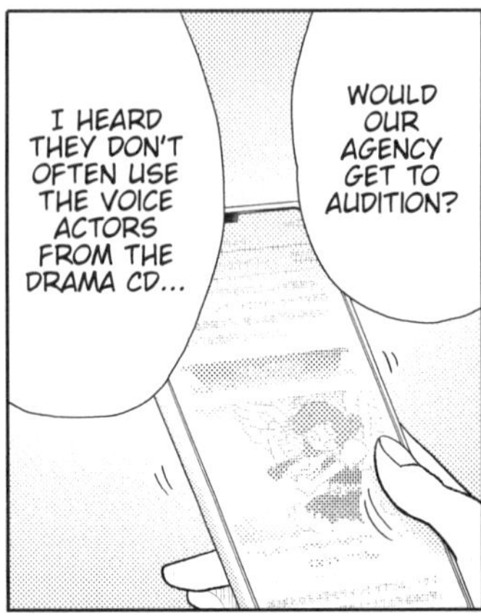
WOULD OUR AGENCY GET TO AUDITION?
I HEARD THEY DON'T OFTEN USE THE VOICE ACTORS FROM THE DRAMA CD...

I AIN'T GONNA LOSE.
WHIIIR
CLUNK
CLUNK
CLUNK
CLUNK

Chapter 36

YURI BAITING?

I'M DATING A GIRL RIGHT NOW!
SO, I CAN DO THIS YURI BAITING THING, TOO, RIGHT?!

SERI-OUSLY?
HUH?
HOOOONK

FWOOOOO
BZZZZZ
BEEP BEEP
WEE WOO
WEE WOO
WEE WOO

THIS IS MY BELOVED SAKUMA. ♡

NICE TO MEET YOU.

NICE TO MEET YOU, TOO!

パ パ パ CLAP CLAP CLAP

OH, BY THE WAY, SENSEI, YOU WORKED ON THE *LATE-NIGHT SCHOOL X* SERIES, RIGHT?
I VOICE ACTED FOR THAT.
YURI BAITING, HUH?
I'VE HEARD ABOUT IT. VOICE ACTRESSES SURE HAVE IT ROUGH.

WE NEVER MET. I WAS STILL A NEWBIE, SO I WAS JUST A MINOR CHARACTER IN THE LAST ORGY.
OH, THEN I GUESS WE'VE MET EACH OTHER BEFORE.
HUH? WAIT A MINUTE ...

JUST HOW MUCH OF AN AIRHEAD IS THIS GIRL?
AH, SO IT'S A SEXY SHOW.
I WONDER IF I CAN GET ONE OF ***THOSE*** ROLES SOMEDAY.
THAT'S BECAUSE IT'S 18+ STUFF.
YOU SHOULD KNOW THIS.
IT'S NOT COMING UP ON WIKI.

I DON'T THINK I CAN TELL YOU ANYTHING HELPFUL.

WE'RE REALLY NOT ALL THAT DIFFERENT FROM A STRAIGHT COUPLE.

SO, YOU HAVE EXPERIENCE WITH MEN, SAKUMA-SAN?

YEAH, THIS IS MY FIRST LESBIAN RELATIONSHIP...

SHE'S REALLY GOOD IN BED, THOUGH.

SERIOUSLY, WHY THE HELL ARE YOU LIKE THIS?!

IN THE END, IT WAS JUST A REGULAR GIRLS-ONLY PARTY.
THANKS FOR THE FOOD!
WERE YOU EXPECTING TO HEAR MORE JUICY DETAILS?
I MEAN, IT'S THEIR PRIVATE LIFE.

WE PROBABLY ALSO SHOULDN'T GIVE OFF TOO MUCH OF THAT VIBE.
MAYBE IT'D BE A GOOD IDEA TO KEEP IT AS "JUST REALLY CLOSE FRIENDS."
YEAH, YEAH.
YOU'RE THINKING TOO HARD ABOUT IT, MIREI.

IT'S NOT THAT BIG OF A DEAL.
REALLY.

NEMORI KYOKO-SAN, VOICE ACTRESS OF THE ELDEST SISTER, AKANE!
WOO!
OU MIREI-SAN, VOICE ACTRESS OF THE SECOND SISTER, SUBARU!
WOO!
MIREI!
NEMO-RIN!
YEEEAH!
MARRY ME!
AND INUZUKA WAKO-SAN...
VOICE ACTRESS OF THE YOUNGEST SISTER, MIDORI!
HELLO, EVERYONE!
CRICKETS...
CHATTER
HUH?
WHO'S SHE?
BEATS ME...
UH...
UM...
CHATTER CHATTER
CHATTER CHATTER
CHATTER
Chapter 37

CHATTER

SSSHH

TAP TAP
トントン
SAKU-MA.
ARE YOU STILL UP?

WHAT'S WRONG?
CAN I HANG OUT WITH YOU?
RATTLE
ガラ…

SURE.
BUT DON'T YOU NEED TO GET UP EARLY?
CREAK
キィーッ…

FWIP
ん
ばっ

ギュッ
SQUEEZE

I HAD...
A SCARY DREAM.

I SEE.

THANK YOU.
YOU MADE ME FEEL A LOT BETTER.

SORRY FOR BOTHERING YOU. GOOD NIGHT!
NIGHT.
THUD

CREAK

ZZZ

Chapter 38
SORRY TO MAKE YOU WAIT!
OH, I JUST GOT HERE.
WANKO-CHAN'S NOT HERE?
WHERE DOES SHE LIVE AGAIN?
SHE TEXTED ME!
SHE MISSED THE TRAIN.
HERE'S THE MENU.
WHAT DID YOU ORDER?
LIKE I SAID, I JUST GOT HERE.
OH.

WHY DON'T WE ORDER THIS?
WE'RE PRETENDING TO BE A COUPLE AND ALL.
季節限定!!
当店特製!!
I ONLY EVER SAW COUPLES DRINK THIS IN ANIME.

WANKO-CHAN'S GIRLFRIEND TOLD US THAT WE...
JUST NEED TO ACT NORMAL.
TSK. HOW BORING.

NORMAL, HUH?
THAT'S RIGHT. JUST ACT NORMAL.
NORMAL... *RIIIGHT...*
NORMAL, NORMAL...

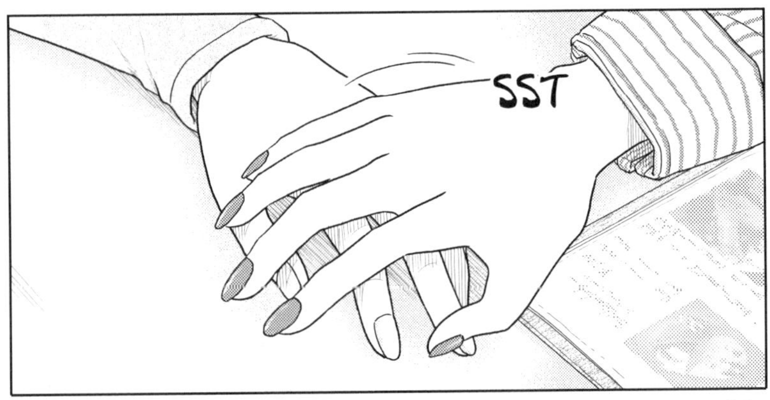
SST

LIKE THIS?
YEAH, WHY NOT?
YOU DON'T MIND LOCKING FINGERS WITH ME?
YEAH, THIS IS FINE.

DO YOU THINK WE...
LOOK LIKE A COUPLE?
OR DOES IT JUST LOOK LIKE WE'RE DOING A CON GAME?
OH, I LEARNED ABOUT THAT.
MY AGENCY BACK THEN HAD TIES WITH THE YAKUZA...

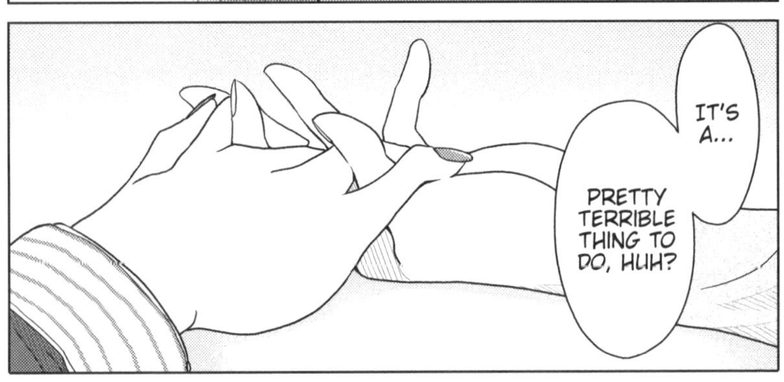

BUT ANYWAY ...
PEOPLE NEED TO RECOGNIZE US WHEN THEY SEE US ON THE STREET.
THAT'S OUR FIRST GOAL.
I GUESS WE'RE STILL NOT AT THAT LEVEL.
WHAT IF WE JUST BECOME AS POPULAR AS MIZU****-SAN?
at ginza.
IF THIS WAS AKIBA, MAYBE.
AKIBA, HUH?

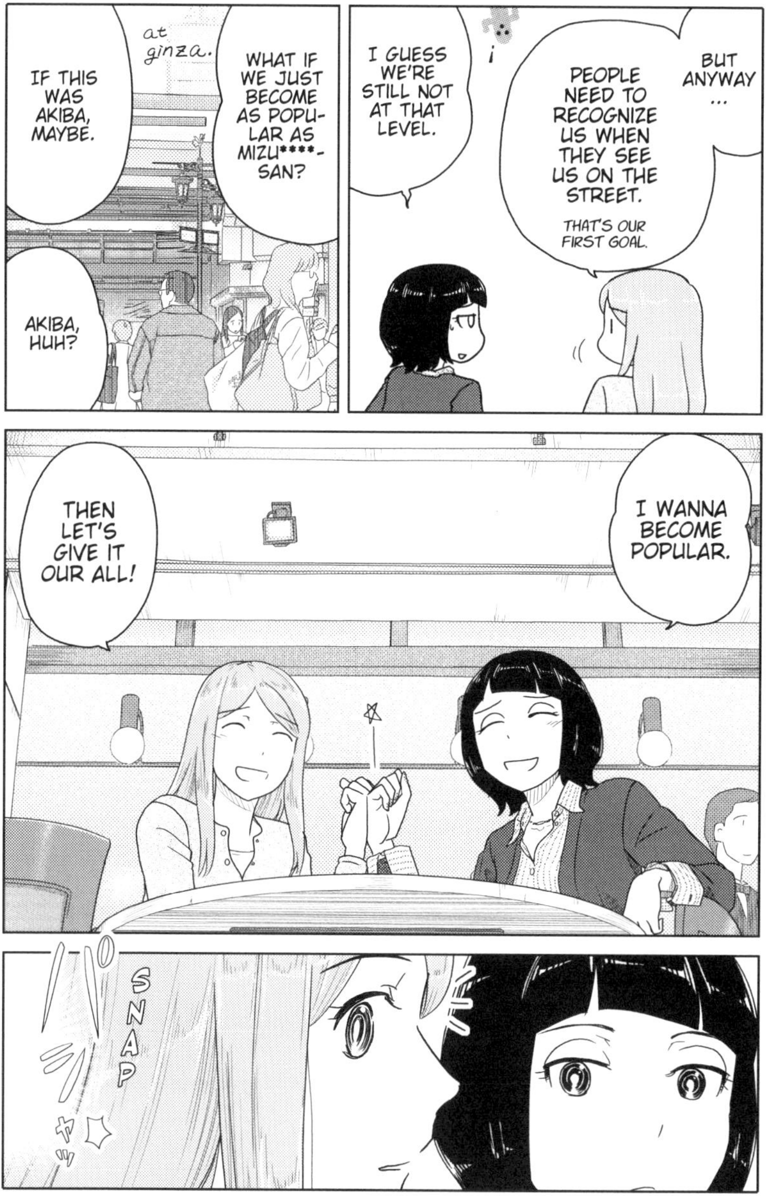

I WANNA BECOME POPULAR.
THEN LET'S GIVE IT OUR ALL!

SNAP

SNAP
SNAP
SNAP

WHO ARE THEY?
ENTERTAINERS, MAYBE?

SO, SOMETHING LIKE THIS?
BASICALLY?
どやーーーん
SMUUUG
NOPE.

Chapter 39

パッ
FLICK

WANKO
?

You're so busy now.
Will you be all right?
They're paying a guar-anteed fee!
I'M INVESTING IN MYSELF!

OH, BUT YOU GOTTA WAIT A BIT LONGER FOR THE RENT.
IT'S OKAY.
I HOPE SHE DOESN'T PUSH HERSELF.

SSSHH
SPLISH
SPLISH

BZZZZZ
WELL THEN ...

WHAT DO I...
DO?
BAM

CHOP

CHOP

CHOP

ENOUGH FOR THREE DAYS. GOES IN THE FRIDGE.

GO-TO FOOD

SIMMERED ROOT VEGETABLES.

CLINK
SSSHH
SSSHH
CLOMP

ZREE
ZREE

SO...

FROM NOW ON...

THERE'LL BE MORE DAYS LIKE THIS.

PLOP

BUT IS THAT RIGHT?

WILL IT GO THAT SMOOTHLY? THIS IS HER ONLY MAIN ROLE SO FAR.

AND IT'S A LATE-NIGHT ANIME AIMED AT ENTHUSIASTS.

SO, LIKE...

ANYWAY...

LET'S TAKE OUT THE TRASH.

ガ
パ
PLUNK

ガサ
RUSTLE

WILL THERE BE MORE DAYS LIKE THIS?

Chapter 40
THANK YOU ALL SO MUCH FOR COMING!
WOOOOOOOO!
WANKOOO!
ISN'T WANKO-CHAN GREAT?
SHE'S LIKE AN AIRHEADED LITTLE SISTER.
IT'S AMAZING HOW MUCH SHE'S IMPROVED AS A VOICE ACTRESS AFTER ONE REGULAR SHOW.
WANKO!
WANKO!
I'VE BEEN KEEPING AN EYE ON HER SINCE THE *SHIMA SHIMA UMAJIRO* DAYS. *HEH HEH HEH!*

GASP!
TWITCH
POP

It's over! Heading home now. ♡
OH.
AWESOME.

WANKO!

WHOA, SAKUMA!
YOU CAME TO GET ME?
IT'S LATE.

SAKUMA...

LOVE
YOU'RE MOVED, I SEE.
HA HA HA!

HOW WAS THE LESSON?

IT WAS PRETTY ROUGH.

I'M DEAD TIRED. I WANNA TAKE A BATH AND SLEEP LIKE A LOG!

I JUST...

WANTED TO GO ON A LITTLE WALK WITH YOU.

THAT'S ALL.

GOSH, SAKUMA!

ARE YOU A GOD OR WHAT?!

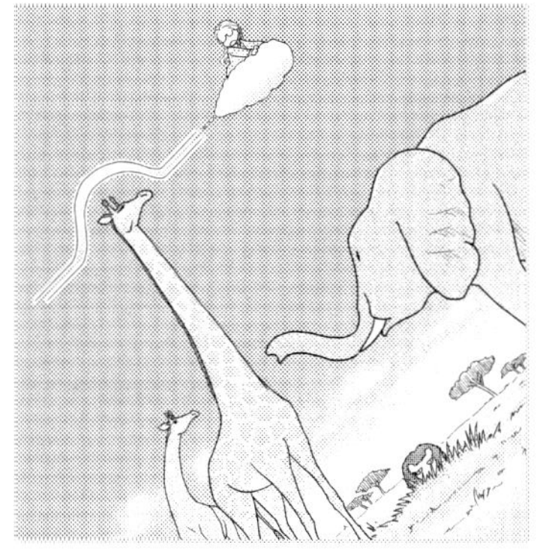

Chapter 41

KA-CHAK
I'M HOME!
WHOA!
WELCOME HOME.
CLEAN-ING YOUR BOOTS?
YEAH.
I'M GOING TO PUT THEM AWAY.
YOU HAVING WRITER'S BLOCK?
UH...
YEAH... SORT OF.

IT'S LIKE WE HAVE A BUNCH OF VISITORS.
AND THEY ALL HAVE GIANT FEET.

YOU ONLY HAVE FLAT SHOES, HUH?
I DON'T THINK I'VE EVER SEEN YOU WEAR HIGH HEELS.
I HAVE A FEW PAIRS, BUT I DON'T WEAR THEM VERY OFTEN, SO THEY JUST GET MOLDY.

DO YOU HAVE ANY SHOES YOU'RE PUTTING AWAY?
I'LL CLEAN THEM FOR YOU.
I DON'T HAVE LEATHER SHOES.

YEAH, I'VE NEVER SEEN YOU WEAR ANY.
THEY JUST HURT MY FEET.

IT'S HARD TO RUN IN THEM, AND THEY GET MOLDY WHEN YOU WEAR THEM ON RAINY DAYS.
WHY DO ADULTS WEAR SUCH INCONVENIENT SHOES?
I MEAN...
MOST ADULTS AREN'T GONNA RUN A LOT IN LEATHER SHOES...
YOU CAN'T WASH THEM, THEY GET SMELLY, AND THEY GIVE YOU BLISTERS!

YOU HAVE THESE SHOES, TOO, SAKUMA?
GRIN

SQUEEK
※ SHE'S ADJUSTING THE SIZE USING PADDING.
THAT SHOULD DO THE TRICK.
IS IT OKAY TO WEAR THEM INDOORS?
I CLEANED THE SOLES, SO IT'S FINE.
IT'D BE DANGEROUS IF YOU TRIPPED OUTSIDE.
CLUNK
R-RIGHT.
TREMBLE
TREMBLE
HMPH!
CLAP CLAP CLAP

WHOA!
STEP
STEP
THIS FEELS KINDA FUNNY.
どたこ
THUNK
OF COURSE.
どたこ
THUNK
BUT...
IT ALSO FEELS KIND OF...
FRESH.
どたこん
THUNK
どたんこ
THUNK
TWIRL くるっ
IT'S LIKE I'VE BECOME A BIT MORE GROWN-UP, I GUESS?
ぐらっ
WOBBLE
WHOA!
CAREFUL!

LOOKS LIKE YOU'LL HAVE TO WEAR THE RIGHT SIZE.
HOW ABOUT WE GO TO A SHOE STORE SOME TIME?
HMM...

THAT CAN WAIT.
YOU SURE?

LOOKING AT THEM IS MORE FUN ANYWAY.

Chapter 42
IT'S THE EARLY 20TH CENTURY IN A CERTAIN COUNTRY IN ASIA!
DR. RYUDOU, AN EMINENT MECHANICAL ENGINEER AND INVENTOR, HAS MYSTERIOUSLY VANISHED!
INHERITING HIS INVENTIONS, HIS THREE BEAUTIFUL DAUGHTERS GO ON AN ADVENTURE ACROSS ASIA, SOLVING MYSTERIES AND FOILING PLOTS ALONG THE WAY!
Coming Soooooon!!
THE THREE SLEUTH SISTERS
HELLOOO!!

TODAY, WE BEGIN A NEW SHOW, *THREE SLEUTH SISTERS RADIO!*
I'M NEMORI KYOKO. I VOICE THE ELDEST SISTER, RYUDOU AKANE!

I'M OU MIREI, AND I VOICE THE SECOND SISTER, RYUDOU SUBARU.
AND LAST BUT NOT LEAST, OUR LITTLE SISTER! THIS'LL BE HER FIRST REGULAR SHOW!

N-NICE TO MEET YOU! I VOICE RYUDOU SUBA--I MEAN MIDORI!
ARE YOU SUBARU OR MIDORI?
WAAAAAAAH!
MIDORI! I VOICE RYUDOU MIDORI! MY NAME IS INUZUKA WAKO! IT'S A PLEASURE TO WORK WITH YOU BOTH!

HEY, SUBARU.
BE NICE TO YOUR SISTER.
HA HA HA.
SORRY, ONEECHAN.
YOU'RE SO MEAN, MIREI-SAN!

NO, I MEAN...
LI'L NEECHAN!
SAAAFE!

BROADCAST WRITER.
NOD NOD
I SEE. LI'L NEECHAN, HUH?
YOU'RE THE YOUNGER BIG SISTER, AFTER ALL.
HI, I'M LI'L NEECHAN (LOL)!
I'M THE LITTLE SISTER! RYUDOU MIDORI!

ANYWAY, THIS RADIO SHOW WILL PROVIDE YOU WITH THE LATEST NEWS ON THE FALL TV ANIME STEAMPUNK ADVENTURE: THE THREE SLEUTH SISTERS, PRODUCED BY STUDIO PONES, DIRECTED BY JAMES KOBAN, AND STARRING US THREE SISTERS! YOU CAN EXPECT US TO BE FUN, DETAILED, AND THOROUGH!
AND ALSO SEXY!
YEAH! WAIT, NO!
Steampunk Adventure
THE THREE SLEUTH SISTERS

NO SEXY STUFF ON THIS SHOW!
GOSH, YOU'RE SUCH A STICK IN THE MUD.
WHAT'S WRONG WITH THAT? WE GOTTA TAKE THIS SERIOUSLY! WE'LL READ MESSAGES FROM OUR LISTENERS, AND HAVE MEMBERS OF THE STAFF AND CAST AS GUESTS ON THE SHOW.

FFT!
EEP!

HEY!
WHAT ARE YOU DOING?! WE'RE LIVE RIGHT NOW!
YOU NEED TO LOOSEN UP, ONEECHAN.
Y-YOU CAN'T DO THAT ON THE SHOW, LI'L NEECHAN!

NO, WE NEED TO DO THIS BECAUSE IT'S THE FIRST EPISODE!

MIDORI, YOU LISTEN, TOO!

IT'S THE FIRST EPISODE, SO WE NEED TO GIVE OUR LISTENERS A DETAILED OVERVIEW OF THE ANIME AND PIQUE THEIR INTEREST!

FFT!

EEP!

SU BA RU ||| !
ONEECHAN, CHILL OUT!
SO, UH...

OUR SHOW WILL BE THIRTY MINUTES OF THIS! THERE'LL BE AN EXTENDED VERSION FOR PEOPLE WITH PAID MEMBERSHIPS, TOO!
WE'LL HAVE A NEW EPISODE FOR YOU EVERY FRIDAY AT NOON, SO...

BE SURE TO TUNE IN!!

Chapter 43

ARE YOU OKAY?!

Y...

YEAH!

HIC!

I'M ALL *RIIIGHT!*

YOU'RE DEAD DRUNK.
SO, HERE'S A FRIENDLY PIECE OF ADVICE. GO HOME!
OH!
YOU SEEM LIKE A GOOD CATCH, LADY! HOW ABOUT A DRINK?
JUST IGNORE HER, ATARU-CHAN.
CLATTER

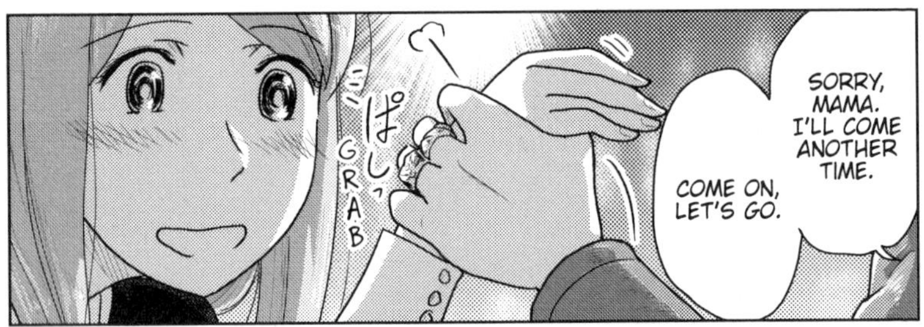
SORRY, MAMA. I'LL COME ANOTHER TIME.
COME ON, LET'S GO.
GRAB

YOU'RE BOTHERING THE OTHER CUSTOMERS.

DON'T TAKE HER HOME FOR A ONE-NIGHT STAND!
I WON'T!

TAXI!
SCREECH
WHERE DO YOU LIVE?
YIPPEE!
OH, DAMN IT!
VROOOM
HEH HEH! WE'RE HAVING A ONE-NIGHT STAND!
WE'RE NOT!

I'M IN LOVE WITH SOMEONE ELSE.
HA HA HA! YOU'RE IN LOVE, HUH?

JUST LIKE ME ...

WE ENDED UP...
ZZZ...
CHIRP
CHEEP CHEEP CHEEP
DOING THE DEED ANYWAY.
WELL, WHAT-EVER.
ELLIE'S GETTING IT ON WITH THAT GIRL, TOO, ISN'T SHE?
NGH ...
MHM ...
WRIGGLE
もぞ...

MORNING.

YOU KNOW...

SHE SURE IS PRETTY.

I WANNA TAKE A SHOWER.

OH, IT SHOULD BE ON THE LEFT...

COME ON, I DON'T KNOW THIS PLACE!

I DON'T KNOW THIS PLACE AT ALL!

I THOUGHT YOU WERE IN LOVE WITH SOMEONE.
SCRUB
わしゃ
SCRUB
わしゃ
YEAH, BUT SHE WOULDN'T HAVE SEX.
SCRUB
わしゃ
AREN'T YOU IN LOVE TOO?
SHE'S GOT A GIRL-FRIEND.
SO, WE'RE IN THE SAME BOAT.
WHY DON'T YOU JUST STEAL HER AWAY? YOU WANT HER, RIGHT?
I JUST DON'T WANT...
TO COMPLICATE THINGS.
YOU'RE SUCH A PURE GAL. ☆
SPLASH
ばしゃっ
I'LL KICK YOU OUT.
NAKED!

Chapter 44

OKAY, GATHER AROUND, NEWBIES!

ALL DEPARTMENTS, PLEASE DO YOUR BEST!

YES, SIR!

YOU WILL BE VERY BUSY HELPING OUT AT THE VENUE, AND YOU MIGHT BE TOO TIRED...

TO EVEN ATTEND THE EVENTS FROM DAY TWO ONWARD, SO I HOPE YOU'RE READY.

STICK THESE TO YOUR DESKS.

YOU MIGHT BE NEWBIES...

BUT EACH OF YOU IS STILL *ONE OF US.*

SO, STAY PROFESSIONAL. THAT'S WHAT MATTERS THE MOST.

BE SURE TO KEEP THAT IN MIND.
YES, SIR!
OH!
I KNOW THIS GIRL.

SHE WAS IN CLASS 2...

Say cheese!

SNAP

WHOSE PHONE IS NEXT?
THERE'S JUST NO END.
WANNA GO TO ROUND ONE AFTER THIS?
Sensei!

I love you, Sensei!

I've loved you all this time!

GO FOR IT!
DON'T RUN AWAY NOW!

Aw!
She got re- jected!

Well, I expect- ed as much.
Well done, Wanko!

IT'S OKAY!
THIS IS PART OF LIFE, TOO!
DON'T LET IT GET YOU DOWN!
パチ
CLAP
パチ
CLAP
パチ
CLAP
パチ
CLAP
パチ
CLAP
パチ
CLAP
パチ
CLAP
パチ
CLAP

WE WERE IN DIFFERENT CLASSES, AND DIDN'T INTERACT MUCH...
BUT SHE HAS A VERY UNIQUE AURA.

Man, that was some good stuff.

Okay, go get changed. We'll meet at 5:30!

SHUFFLE SHUFFLE

SO SHE...
BECAME A VOICE ACTRESS, HUH?
East Hall Blue Stage - 15:30-18:10
Neo Western
WOW...
THIS ANIME SEEMS PRETTY HUGE.
PEOPLE LIKE **HER** ARE JUST...
BORN WITH **THAT** KIND OF THING.
Steampunk Adventure

Chapter 45
A LITTLE WHILE AGO...
HAPPY BIRTHDAY...
TO YOU!
HAPPY BIRTHDAY...
TO YOU!
HAPPY BIRTHDAY...
DEAR WANKO!
HAPPY BIRTHDAY...
TO YOU!
HERE YOU GO.
SAKUMA
佐久
LOVE

Is there anything you want, Sakuma?
My birthday is still a ways off.
I'll save up for it!
No, there's no need.
I WANT TO GIVE YOU A PRESENT!
Hmm...
Then...
I'd like a roommate who passes her audition and pays the rent.
Kgh!
ぎんっ
GRIT
HA HA HA! JUST KIDDING.
JEEZ, SAKUMA!
I SAID THAT AND ALL, BUT SHE...
ACTUALLY PASSED HER AUDITION.
THE RENT STILL HAS TO WAIT, THOUGH.
SIP

SHE MUST BE SUPER BUSY.
FFT...

SHE HASN'T ASKED ME ABOUT IT SINCE THEN.
OR MAYBE SHE JUST FORGOT? WELL, I HAVEN'T TALKED MUCH ABOUT IT, EITHER...
SIP
POP

Done with rehearsal for the stage show. Having dinner now.

PLAN ① BLAME EVERYTHING ON AGE.
HEIGH-HO!
OH, DEAR ME. I'M GETTING ON IN YEARS.
GASP!
COME TO THINK OF IT, IT'S ALMOST HER BIRTHDAY!
BUT I FEEL KIND OF SORRY FOR HER, SO I'LL PRETEND I FORGOT!
HMM...

PLAN ② OBSESS OVER THE CALENDAR.
OH, IT'S ALMOST HERE!
IT'S ALMOST TIME FOR THAT!
GLANCE
GLANCE
GASP!
OH YEAH, MY ANIME WILL BE AIRING SOON!
SHE'S LOOKING FORWARD TO IT THAT MUCH, HUH? I LOVE YOU, SAKUMA!
HMM...

PLAN ③ JUST BE DIRECT ABOUT IT.
BY THE WAY, ISN'T IT...
ABOUT TIME YOU PAY THE RENT?
GASP!
IS SAKUMA GETTING LESS WORK?!
DON'T WORRY! I'LL WORK HARDER AND GET MANY MORE REGULAR ROLES!
HMM-MMM...

AAAH! SAKUMA!
TODAY IS YOUR BIRTHDAY!

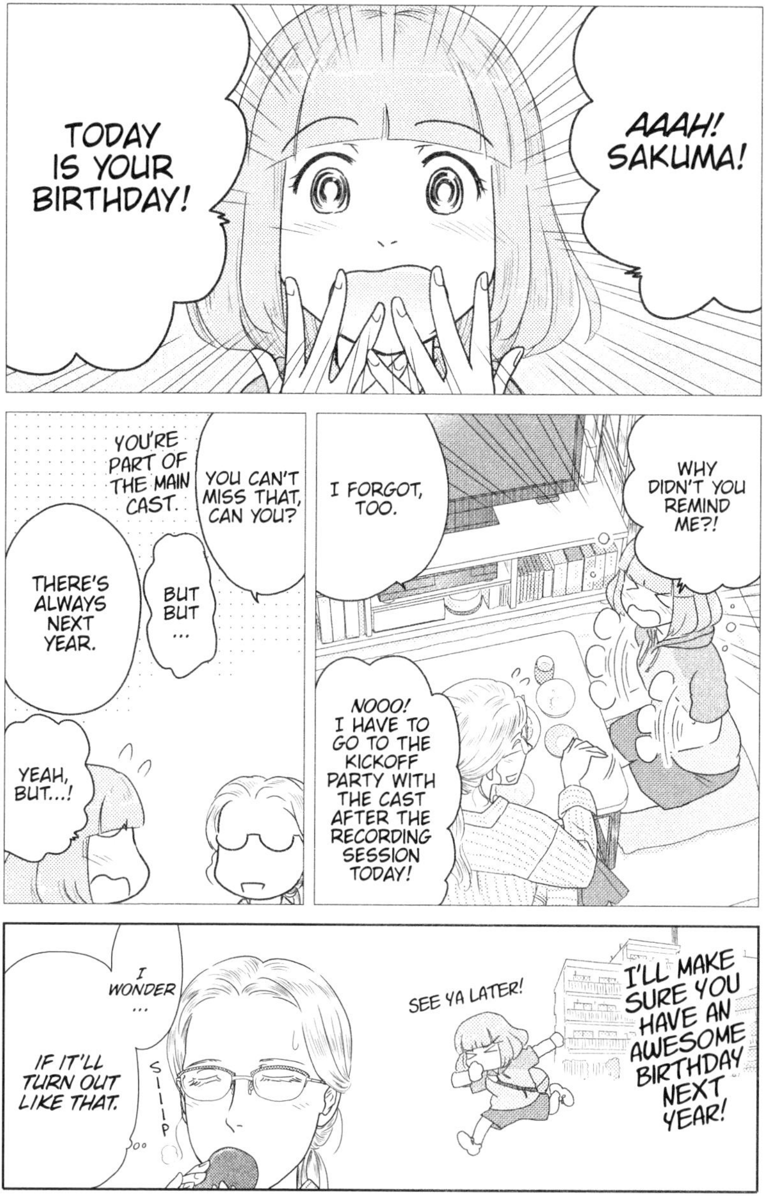

WHY DIDN'T YOU REMIND ME?!
I FORGOT, TOO.
NOOO! I HAVE TO GO TO THE KICKOFF PARTY WITH THE CAST AFTER THE RECORDING SESSION TODAY!
YOU CAN'T MISS THAT, CAN YOU?
YOU'RE PART OF THE MAIN CAST.
BUT BUT ...
THERE'S ALWAYS NEXT YEAR.
YEAH, BUT...!

I'LL MAKE SURE YOU HAVE AN AWESOME BIRTHDAY NEXT YEAR!
SEE YA LATER!
I WONDER ...
IF IT'LL TURN OUT LIKE THAT.
SLIIP

I GUESS IT'S ABOUT TIME I TAKE ON A BIG JOB.

MAYBE.

CREAK

Chapter 46
I KINDA GOT THE FEELING...

THAT IT MIGHT JUST BE THE CASE.

WE'RE...
FRIENDS, AFTER ALL.

I REMEMBER MEETING HER FOR THE FIRST TIME AT WORK.
SHE WAS VERY CALM FOR A NEWBIE, SO SHE STOOD OUT.

SHE WAS A COLLEGE GRAD WHO FAILED HER ENTRANCE EXAM ONCE, SO I TOLD HER NOT TO TAKE BIG RISKS.

HUH...

BUT REALLY, WHO AM I TO CRITICIZE ANYONE'S CAREER CHOICES?

WE WERE BOTH MISFITS, SO WE GOT ALONG WELL.
WE EVEN HUNG OUT TOGETHER WHEN WE WEREN'T WORKING.

Let's see who'll voice a Pretty C*re first!
I'd rather be one of the villains.

I THOUGHT THAT MAYBE SHE ACTUALLY HATED ME.

Ou Mirei

Ou Mirei Google search
Ou Mirei former agency
Ou Mirei name change
Ou Mirei sex scandal
Ou Mirei plastic surgery
Ou Mirei bad voice acting

I MEAN, MY PREVIOUS AGENCY DID SOME BAD STUFF. IT WAS IN THE NEWS, TOO.

I'll probably get a mom role first!
Shit! That is pretty likely...

I WAS SUCH A FOOL.
I'M SO ASHAMED I DOUBTED HER.

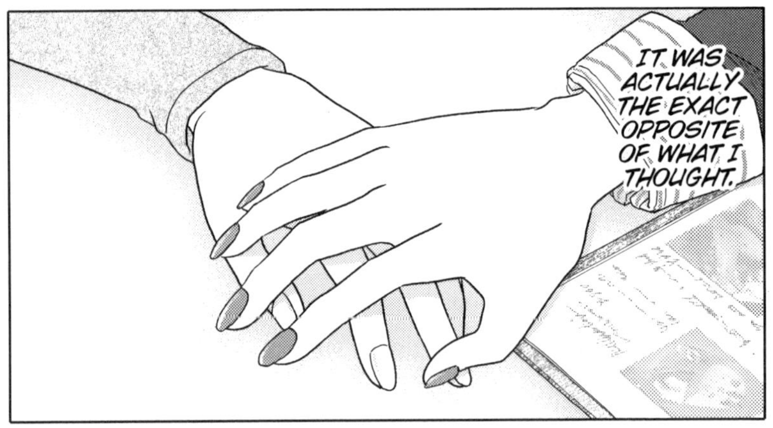
IT WAS ACTUALLY THE EXACT OPPOSITE OF WHAT I THOUGHT.

SORRY, KYOKO.
I WANT TO STAY FRIENDS.

THAT'S WHY THIS IS...
THE LEAST I CAN DO.

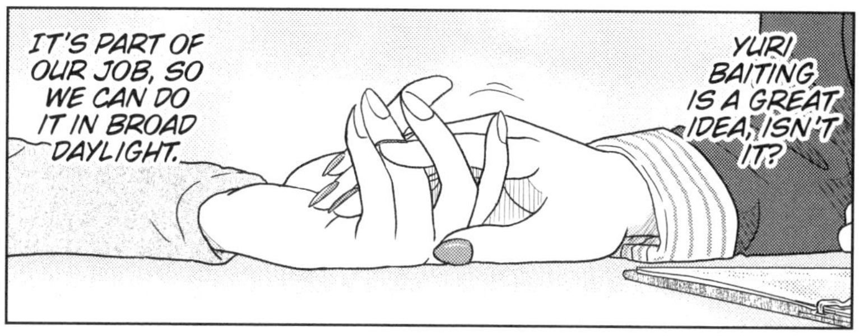
YURI BAITING IS A GREAT IDEA, ISN'T IT?
IT'S PART OF OUR JOB, SO WE CAN DO IT IN BROAD DAYLIGHT.

COME ON, KYOKO.
YOU CAN PUT THE MOVES ON ME, TOO.

AN AWFUL THING TO DO, HUH?

IT REALLY IS...

SHUDDER SHUDDER
DON'T SAY THAT WITH SUCH A SEXY FACE!
SHE'S CLEARLY AWAKENED TO SOME-THING.
AAAAAAH!
SHUDDER SHUDDER SHUDDER
SHUDDER SHUDDER SHUDDER

Chapter 47

I OVER-SLEPT!
SORRY, SAKUMA! I GOTTA GO!
うわーーん
WAAAAAH!
UP ALL NIGHT.
TAKE CARE.
TMP TMP TMP TMP TMP
ガチャ
KA-CHAK
THUD
SERIOUSLY?
TODAY IS MY BIRTHDAY, BUT SHE DIDN'T SAY A THING ABOUT IT.
WELL...
I ALSO TRIED TO ACT LIKE I DON'T CARE...
BUT STILL...

Yeah ☆
BIRTH-DAY!
HAPPY!
HAPPY...
POP POP POP POP
THUD THUD THUD THUD
THUMP
SST
WE'RE HERE TO...
TALK ABOUT THE SCRIPT, RIGHT?
CHATTER
CHATTER CHATTER
CHATTER

WHISPER
HEY.
DID SOMETHING HAPPEN WITH WANKO?
NO.
NOTHING HAPPENED.
SHE PROBABLY JUST FORGOT, SINCE SHE'S NEVER BEEN THIS BUSY.
AND AFTER ALL...
THAT'S GOOD. SO I'M FINE WITH IT.
SMACK!
GLOOOOM

プポポポ…
PUTT PUTT PUTT
I'LL DRIVE YOU HOME.

YOU'VE BEEN LIVING TOGETHER FOR, WHAT, A YEAR AND A HALF?
IT'S ABOUT TIME FOR THAT TO HAPPEN.
PUTT
PUTT
PUTT
PUTT
PUTT

V R E E E E
WELL...

I'M NOT SAYING YOUR RELATIONSHIP IS GONNA GO SOUR, OKAY?!
YEAH, I KNOW.

AT SOME POINT, EVERY-THING...

JUST STOPS BEING SPECIAL, HUH?

THAT'S JUST HOW LIVING TOGETHER IS.

PUTT PUTT PUTT PUTT
PSSK!

THANK YOU...
FOR GOING OUT OF YOUR WAY TO DRIVE ME HOME.
DON'T WORRY ABOUT IT.

THIS IS...
JUST HOW THINGS HAVE ALWAYS BEEN BETWEEN US.

SST

THAT'S IT?

Wanko

Sorry about this morning!

It happens.

Done recording!

Nice! I still have work.

Finally done! Heading home.

Happy Birthday!

Chapter 48
KA-CHAK
ガチャン…

ゴォ
FWOOO

I'M HOME
...

Sorry about this morning!
It happens.
Done recording!
Nice! I still have work.
Finally done! Heading home.
Happy Birthday!

WELL...
SHE'S BUSY, AFTER ALL...
TMP

どたっ
THUD
OW!
ガッ
TRIP
カラララッ
RATTLE

HAPPY BIRTHDAY...

TO YOU!

♪

HAPPY BIRTHDAY...

TO YOU!

HAPPY BIRTHDAY...

DEAR...

SAKUMA!

SAKUMA!
HAPPY BIRTHDAY!
I'M YOUR PRESENT.
BA-BAAAM

WAN...
KO.
WHOOSH
THUD
SORRY, I GOTTA USE THE BATHROOM!
I HAD THE PERFECT SURPRISE PLANNED FOR YOU, BUT THEN I HEARD ATARU'S CAR...
HAVE FUN, YOU TWO!
AND TO TOP IT OFF, YOU TRIPPED AT THE ENTRANCE. WAY TO RUIN IT!
YOU'RE NOT YOUNG ANYMORE! GOTTA CUT DOWN ON THE ALL-NIGHTERS!
OKAY, OKAY.
I'M YOUR PRESENT.
SHE SURPRISED SAKUMA, BUT STILL COULDN'T PAY THE RENT.

The Two of Them Are Pretty Much Like This

To be continued in Volume 3

The Two of Them Are Pretty Much Like This One-Page Bonus

The 1/7 Plan

Thank you for purchasing this manga! Takashi Ikeda 2021 Feb

SEVEN SEAS ENTERTAINMENT PRESENTS

The Two of Them Are Pretty Much Like This

story and art by **TAKASHI IKEDA** **VOL. 2**

TRANSLATION
Anh Kiet Ngo

LETTERING
Rina Mapa

COVER DESIGN
H. Qi

PROOFREADER
Krista Grandy

SENIOR COPY EDITOR
Dawn Davis

EDITOR
Linda Lombardi

PRODUCTION DESIGNER
Christina McKenzie

PRODUCTION MANAGER
Lissa Pattillo

PREPRESS TECHNICIAN
Melanie Ujimori

PRINT MANAGER
Rhiannon Rasmussen-Silverstein

EDITOR-IN-CHIEF
Julie Davis

ASSOCIATE PUBLISHER
Adam Arnold

PUBLISHER
Jason DeAngelis

Seven Seas press and purchase enquiries can be sent to Marketing Manager Lianne Sentar at press@gomanga.com. Information regarding the distribution and purchase of digital editions is available from Digital Manager CK Russell at digital@gomanga.com.

ISBN: 978-1-63858-296-0
Printed in USA
First Printing: November 2022
10 9 8 7 6 5 4 3 2 1

READING DIRECTIONS

This book reads from *right to left*, Japanese style. If this is your first time reading manga, you start reading from the top right panel on each page and take it from there. If you get lost, just follow the numbered diagram here. It may seem backwards at first, but you'll get the hang of it! Have fun!!

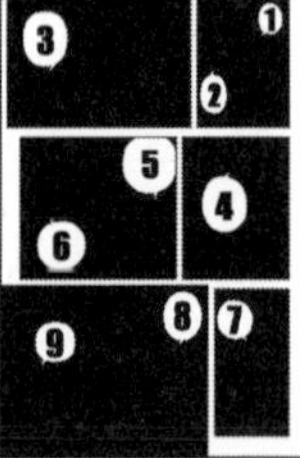

Follow us online: www.SevenSeasEntertainment.com